Your Gluten Free Cookie Jar

40 Cookie Recipes You Won't Believe Are Gluten Free!

By Bridget Towery

Printed in the United States of America

Second Printing, 2018

ISBN-13: 978-1540463210

ISBN-10: 1540463214

CreateSpace Independent Publishing Platform
North Charleston, South Carolina

Edited by: Christina Lynne

Photo Credits

Fotolia Images: pp. 13, 21, 26, 33, 35, 37, 43, 57, 59, 75
Bigstock Images: pp. 28, 29, 47, 60, 65, 71, 73, 83

Dedication & Acknowledgements

For Linda Lee Peterson

Thank you to my husband, Brian, for your patience and loving support through our gluten-free journey.

To my son, Jimmy: thank you for always making me laugh!

To my granddaughter, Kinsley: thank you for being Nana's baking buddy!

I am especially thankful for my friend and fellow author, Beverly Bradley, for your expertise!

Summer Simmons-Turpin, thank you for your never ending encouragement.

Christina Lynne, thank you for the many brainstorming sessions!

Table of Contents

Introduction

Are you looking for delicious gluten-free cookie recipes? I am here to tell you that you can make them with the same fresh-from-the-oven aroma, wonderful tastes and textures that remind you of visits to Grandma's house.

After becoming gluten-free in 2009, I remember the dismal feeling that my love for baking was going to be a distant memory. Instead, a whole new world was waiting for me.

After trying a lot of gluten-free cookie mixes and being extremely disappointed, I began researching baking without gluten. After many trials and errors (not to mention a lot of money,) I found a gluten-free almond flour blend that measures cup-for-cup to regular wheat flour. It makes converting recipes so much easier. I like being able to purchase one kind of flour instead of several different ones. Not only does it save money; it also saves storage space. With just a few exceptions, I use **Gluten Free Mama's Almond Blend Flour** for all of my baking. With this brand, my cookies are always fluffy and full of flavor!

Finding the flour was just one part of the equation. You may notice that I use a very small amount of xanthan gum in my recipes. This binder allows my baked goods to stay together without having a gritty texture or unpleasant after taste. I buy an eight ounce bag of xanthan gum and it lasts about two years stored in the refrigerator.

I have taken all of my favorite cookie recipes and converted them to gluten-free. So many people tell me after trying my cookies they "can't believe it's gluten-free."

I believe every home should have a cookie jar filled with delicious homemade cookies. It is a wonderful way to create life-long memories for your children and grandchildren;

memories that will be cherished for years to come every time they bake a batch of cookies.

If you enjoy my baked goods, please visit my blog at www.bakingwithbridget.com for even more tips, tricks and recipes!

Happy Baking!

Bridget

Baking Equipment Supply List

~ Stand mixer or hand held mixer

~ Baking sheets (without sides) and oblong baking dish

~ Cooling racks

~ Parchment paper or silicone baking mat

~ Mixing bowls, measuring cups and spoons

~ Cookie spatula and rolling pin

~ Flour Sifter

~ Plastic wrap

~ Pot holders, dish towels

~ Cookie cutters, cookie press and icing bag with tips.

Bar Cookies

Best Raspberry Bars

Dark Chocolate Brownies

Magic Cookie Bars

Frosted Pumpkin Bars

Cut these cookies into bars or squares.

Apple Caramel Crumb Bars

If you love apples and caramel, you will love these delicious bars! Made with homemade caramel, they are simply divine!

Makes 12-15 bars

Ingredients for crust/crumb topping:

2 $^2/_3$ cups gluten-free almond blend flour
1 $^2/_3$ cups oats, quick cooking
1 cup brown sugar, firmly packed
$^1/_4$ teaspoon sea salt
Pinch of xanthan gum
1 cup unsalted butter, melted
2 cups Granny Smith apples, peeled and chopped

Ingredients for caramel:

2 cups cane sugar
1 cup brown sugar
1 cup light corn syrup
1 cup sweetened condensed milk
1 cup whole milk
$^1/_3$ cup butter
$^1/_4$ teaspoon sea salt
2 teaspoons vanilla extract

Directions:

Preheat oven to 350° F. Grease a 9x13 inch baking pan.

Combine flour, oats, sugar, salt and xanthan gum in a large bowl. Stir in butter until mixture is crumbly. **Firmly press half the crust/crumb topping mixture (1$^1/_3$ cup) evenly into the pan**. Set aside.

Mix cane and brown sugars, corn syrup, condensed milk and whole milk in a heavy 3-quart saucepan.

Cook over medium heat, stirring occasionally until sugars are dissolved and syrup starts to boil. Reduce heat to low. Stir occasionally to prevent scorching until mixture reads 240° on candy thermometer. Cook and stir constantly until firm ball stage (246° F to 248° F.) Remove pan from heat.

Stir in butter and salt until well blended. Stir in vanilla until thoroughly blended.

Toss apples with 3 tablespoons of gluten free flour and spread over mixture in pan. Pour caramel evenly over apples. Top with remaining crust/crumb topping. Press topping lightly onto apples and caramel.

Bake until golden brown and apples are tender, 25 to 30 minutes. Cut into bars while warm. Let cool completely. **Cover and refrigerate 6 hours or overnight before serving.**

Bridget's Baking Tip: Save time by purchasing a bag of caramels and melting them in a double boiler.

Best Ever Raspberry Bars

The coconut adds a tropical flavor to these homemade bars. Perfect all year round!

Makes 16 large bars

Ingredients:

$^3/_4$ cup unsalted butter, softened
$^3/_4$ cup brown sugar, packed
$^1/_4$ cup cane sugar
1 cup gluten-free almond flour blend
$1^1/_2$ cups old-fashioned oatmeal, gluten free
2 cups unsweetened coconut, divided
1 jar raspberry preserves

Directions:

Preheat oven to 375° F.

Beat butter, brown sugar and cane sugar in large mixing bowl until creamy. Stir in flour, oatmeal and 1 cup of coconut, mixing well. Set aside 1 of dough.

Press remainder of dough evenly in bottom of 9x13 inch baking dish. Spread raspberry preserves over the dough. Crumble remaining dough over the preserves. Sprinkle remaining one cup of coconut over the dough.

Bake for 25 minutes or until golden brown. Remove from oven. Allow to cool completely and cut into squares.

Homemade Vanilla Recipe

**7-9 Madagascar vanilla beans
1 cup alcohol (rum or vodka)**

Slice vanilla beans down middle and gently scrape inside of pod. Place in an 8 ounce glass jar.

Pour one cup alcohol over beans until they are covered. Add lid.

Place in back of dark cabinet. Shake jar once per day for two weeks.

Butterscotch Brownies

Bet you can't eat just one of these rich treats!

Makes 16 large brownies

Ingredients:

$1/4$ cup shortening
1 cup brown sugar, packed
1 teaspoon vanilla extract
1 large egg
$3/4$ cup gluten-free almond blend flour
1 teaspoon baking powder
$1/2$ teaspoon sea salt
$1/8$ teaspoon xanthan gum

Directions:

Preheat oven to 350° F. Grease a square 8x8 inch pan.

Heat shortening in a small saucepan over low heat until melted. Remove from heat.

Mix together melted shortening, brown sugar, vanilla and egg in a large bowl.

Sift together flour, baking powder, sea salt and xanthan gum. Stir into wet mixture until just combined. Spread in greased pan.

Bake 25 to 30 minutes. Let cool until just warm. Cut into squares.

Bridget's Baking Tip: For a delicious dessert, serve brownies warm with a dollop of vanilla ice cream and drizzle with chocolate syrup.

Coconut Pecan Bars

Moist and chewy, these bars will remind you of pecan pie.

Makes 16 large bars

Ingredients for crust:

$^1/_2$ cup unsalted butter, softened
$^1/_2$ cup light brown sugar, packed
1 cup gluten-free almond blend flour

Ingredients for filling:

2 large eggs, beaten
1 cup light brown sugar, packed
$1^1/_2$ teaspoons vanilla extract
3 tablespoons gluten-free almond blend flour
1 teaspoon baking powder
$^1/_4$ teaspoon baking soda
1 cup pecan pieces
1 cup shredded coconut

Directions for crust:

Preheat oven to 350° F.

Combine butter, brown sugar and flour in a small bowl.
Press into a 9x13 inch baking dish. Bake for 12 to 15
minutes or until light brown.

Combine all filling ingredients in a large bowl. Spread filling
over baked crust.

Bake again for 25 to 30 minutes or until golden brown. Cool
completely and cut into squares.

Dark Chocolate Brownies

Incredibly moist, these brownies are in season all year!

Makes 16 brownies

Ingredients:

$2/3$ cup unsalted butter, softened
5 1-ounce squares of dark chocolate, cut into pieces
$1^3/_4$ cups cane sugar
2 teaspoons vanilla extract
3 large eggs
1 cup gluten-free almond blend flour
$1/_8$ teaspoon xanthan gum
1 cup chopped nuts, optional

Directions:

Preheat oven to 350° F. Grease a 9x9 inch pan.

Heat the butter and chocolate in a small saucepan over low heat. Stir constantly until melted. Remove from heat and cool 5 minutes.

Beat the sugar, vanilla and eggs in a large mixing bowl on high speed for 5 minutes. Beat in butter and chocolate mixture on low speed until combined.

Sift together the flour and xanthan gum in a small bowl. Mix in flour to sugar/egg mixture until just blended. Stir in nuts, if desired. Spread batter in greased pan.

Bake just until brownies start to pull away from sides of pan, 45 to 50 minutes. Cool completely before cutting.

Homemade Eggnog Recipe

10 eggs
3/4 cup confectioners' sugar
2 cups whole milk
2 cups heavy whipping cream
1/2 teaspoon ground cinnamon
1/2 teaspoon ground nutmeg

Separate eggs. Beat egg yolks in a large bowl. Slowly add sugar. Refrigerate mixture until chilled.

Stir in milk, cinnamon and nutmeg 30 minutes before serving.

In a large bowl, beat egg whites until stiff. Fold into the egg mixture.

In a medium size bowl, beat heavy cream until it forms stiff peaks. Do not overbeat. Gently fold the whipped cream into the egg mixture. Garnish with ground nutmeg.

Delightful Eggnog Bars

If you are a fan of eggnog, you will love these rich and creamy bar cookies.

Makes 16 bars

Ingredients:

$1/2$ cup unsalted butter, softened
1 cup gluten-free almond blend flour
$3/4$ cup cane sugar
5 large egg yolks
$1^1/4$ cups whipping cream, heavy
1 tablespoon rum or 1 teaspoon rum extract
$3/4$ teaspoon ground nutmeg

Directions:

Preheat oven to 350° F. Line bottom and sides of 9x9 inch square pan with parchment paper or aluminum foil. Be sure the paper or foil extends 2 inches over opposite sides of pan.

Mix butter, flour and half a cup of the sugar in a small bowl. Press in bottom and up the sides (about $1/2$ inch) of pan. Bake 20 minutes.

Reduce oven temperature to **300° F.** In a medium bowl, beat egg yolks and remaining sugar with electric mixer, on medium high speed, until mixture is thick. Gradually beat in whipping cream, rum and $1/4$ teaspoon nutmeg. Pour over crust.

Bake 40 to 50 minutes longer or until custard is set and a knife inserted in center comes out clean. Cool completely. Sprinkle tops of bars with remaining nutmeg. Lift foil out of pan. Cut into bars. Store covered in refrigerator.

Frosted Pumpkin Bars

These incredibly moist bars would be perfect to serve for brunch or a simple dessert after supper.

Makes 16 large bars

Ingredients:

2 cups of cane sugar
4 large eggs
2 cups gluten-free almond blend flour
2 tablespoons baking powder
1 teaspoon baking soda
$1/2$ teaspoon pumpkin pie spice
$1/4$ teaspoon cinnamon
$1/8$ teaspoon xanthan gum
$3/4$ cup unsalted butter, melted
2 cups canned pumpkin
1 cup raisins, optional
1 cup walnuts, optional

Directions:

Preheat oven to 325° F. Grease 9x13 inch glass baking dish.

Cream sugar and eggs together in large mixing bowl.

Sift the dry ingredients together in a medium size bowl. Add melted butter, pumpkin and dry ingredients into creamed mixture. Beat until well mixed. Stir in raisins and/or walnuts, if desired. Spread the thick batter evenly into baking dish.

Bake 25 minutes or until a toothpick inserted in the middle comes out clean. Cool and frost with cream cheese frosting recipe on next page.

Cream Cheese Frosting I

Ingredients:

3 ounce cream cheese
6 tablespoons unsalted butter, softened
1 tablespoon vanilla
1 tablespoon milk
2 cups confectioners' sugar

Directions:

Combine the above ingredients in a medium size mixing bowl. Beat three minutes or until creamy. If the frosting is too thick, add in $^1/_4$ teaspoon milk until spreadable consistency is reached.

Bridget's Baking Tip: For perfectly baked cookies, know your oven temperature. Oven thermometers take out the guessing.

Jean's Zucchini Brownies

You won't believe how moist these brownies are. They are a great way to use those extra zucchini from the garden.

Makes 12-16 large or 24 small brownies

Ingredients:

2 cups fresh zucchini, grated
$1^1/_4$ cups sugar
$^1/_2$ cup avocado oil
2 teaspoons vanilla
2 cups gluten-free almond flour
$^1/_4$ cup baking cocoa
$1^1/_2$ teaspoons baking soda
1 teaspoon sea salt
1 teaspoon ground cinnamon
$^1/_8$ teaspoon xanthan gum

Directions:

Preheat oven to 350° F.

Combine zucchini, sugar, oil and vanilla in a large bowl.

Sift together flour, cocoa, baking soda, sea salt, cinnamon and xanthan gum. Mix thoroughly with wet ingredients. Pour into greased 9x13 inch baking dish.

Bake for 25 to 35 minutes or until a toothpick inserted in middle comes out clean. Remove from oven and completely cool. Sprinkle with sifted confectioners' sugar or frost, if desired.

Bridget's Baking Tip: *Confectioners' sugar and powdered sugar are the same.*

18

Rich Hot Chocolate Recipe

2 cups whole milk
2 3/4 Tablespoons cane sugar
3 Tablespoons cocoa
Pinch of sea salt
1/8 teaspoon extract

In a medium saucepan, heat milk, sugar, cocoa and sea salt over medium low heat. Stir constantly until heated. Remove from heat and stir in vanilla extract.

Garnish with homemade whipped cream or marshmallows.

Magic Cookie Bars

This gluten-free version is just as yummy as its gluten laden cousin. It is a family favorite for the holidays.

Makes about 16 bars

Ingredients:

$^1/_3$ cup unsalted butter
$1^1/_3$ cups gluten-free graham cracker crumbs
1 can (14 ounce) sweetened condensed milk
1 cup semi-sweet chocolate chips
1 cup butterscotch chips
$1^1/_3$ cup coconut, flaked

Directions:

Preheat oven to 350° F.

Melt butter in a 9x13 inch baking pan in the oven. Sprinkle graham cracker crumbs over melted butter. Pour condensed milk over crumbs. Top with remaining ingredients. Firmly, but gently, press down with fork.

Bake 25 minutes or until lightly browned. Cool completely and cut into bars.

Bridget's Baking Tip: *Bar cookies are great for large gatherings and potlucks.*

Cookie Tips

Before you start baking be sure to:

~ read through the recipe

~ gather the ingredients

~ collect necessary utensils

~ heat the oven

~measure the ingredients

DROP COOKIES

Cran Orange Cookies

Grandma's Oatmeal Cookies

Summer's Pumpkin Cookies

Best Meringue Cookies

"Baking cookies is comforting, and cookies are the sweetest little bit of comfort food." ~ Sandra Lee

Applesauce Cookies

An old fashioned, moist cookie that tastes like applesauce cake!

Makes 6 dozen cookies

Ingredients:

$^1/_2$ cup unsalted butter, softened
$1^1/_2$ cups brown sugar, packed
2 large eggs
2 tablespoons milk
$2^3/_4$ cups gluten-free almond blend flour
1 teaspoon salt
1 teaspoon ground cinnamon
$^1/_2$ teaspoon baking soda
$^1/_4$ teaspoon ground cloves
$^1/_8$ teaspoon xanthan gum
$^3/_4$ cup applesauce
1 teaspoon vanilla

Directions:

Preheat oven to 375° F. Line cookie sheets with a baking mat or parchment paper.

Cream together the butter and sugar in large bowl. Add eggs one at a time followed by milk, blend thoroughly.

Sift flour, salt, cinnamon, baking soda, cloves and xanthan gum together in a medium size bowl. Add to wet mixture. Stir until combined. Stir in applesauce and vanilla until blended. Drop dough by rounded teaspoonful 1-inch apart on cookie sheet.

Bake 8 to 10 minutes. Immediately remove from cookie sheet to wire rack to cool completely.

Best Meringue Cookies

Rich in vanilla taste, the meringue keeps these dainty gems light and airy. Crisp on the outside, they literally melt in your mouth.

Makes 4 to 5 dozen cookies

Ingredients:

3 egg whites
$^1/_4$ teaspoon cream of tartar
$1^1/_2$ teaspoons vanilla extract
Pinch of salt
$^2/_3$ cup of cane sugar

Directions:

Place egg whites in a medium bowl. Let stand at room temperature for 30 minutes.

Preheat oven to 250° F. Line baking sheets with a baking mat or parchment paper.

Add cream of tartar, vanilla and salt to egg whites. Beat on medium speed until foamy. Gradually add sugar (**1 tablespoon at a time**) beating on high-speed after each addition, until sugar is completely dissolved. Continue beating on high until stiff glossy peaks form, about 5 to 7 minutes.

Cut a small hole in the tip of a disposable pastry bag and insert a #32 star tip. Gently spoon the meringue into the pastry bag. Pipe out cookies (1 $^1/_4$-inch diameter) about 2 inches apart.

Bake 40-45 minutes or until firm to the touch. Turn off the oven (do not open oven door); **leave meringues in oven for approximately 1 hour.** This allows the cookies to cool without cracking.

Remove meringues from oven and let cool completely on baking sheets. Remove cookies from parchment paper and store in a cookie jar or an airtight container.

Bridget's Cookie Tip: *Make these sweet little cookies extra special by adding a drop or two of food coloring. Pink and light green are perfect for spring teas, bridal showers and baby showers.*

Chewy Oatmeal Butterscotch Cookies

I always made these chewy cookies for my dad. He loved the rich buttery flavor. Make them extra special by drizzling melted chocolate across the top.

Makes about 4 dozen cookies

Ingredients:

$1^1/_4$ cups gluten-free almond blend flour, plus 3 tablespoons
1 teaspoon baking soda
$^1/_2$ teaspoon ground cinnamon
$^1/_2$ teaspoon salt
$^1/_8$ teaspoon xanthan gum
1 cup unsalted butter, softened
$^3/_4$ cup cane sugar
$^3/_4$ cup brown sugar, packed
2 large eggs
1 teaspoon vanilla extract
1 teaspoon orange peel, grated
3 cups old-fashioned oats, gluten-free
$1^2/_3$ cups butterscotch chips, gluten-free

Directions:

Preheat oven to 375° F. Line two baking sheets with a baking mat or parchment paper.

Sift together flour, baking soda, cinnamon, salt and xanthan gum in a small size bowl. Set aside.

Beat butter and sugars together in a medium size bowl until creamy. Add in eggs one at a time and mix thoroughly. Mix in vanilla and orange peel.

Mix in flour mixture, one cup at a time. Stir in oats and butterscotch chips. **Chill 10 minutes.** Drop by rounded tablespoons onto prepared baking sheets.

Bake 9 to 10 minutes or until cookies are brown around edges.

Remove from oven and let sit on cookie sheet about 5 minutes. Move cookies to wire rack and cool completely.

Bridget's Baking Tip: Gluten-free cookies need a binder, such as xanthan gum, to prevent them from crumbling.

Chocolate Chip Cookies

They are delicious served warm with a glass of milk.

Makes about 4 dozen cookies

Ingredients:

1 cup unsalted butter, softened
1 cup cane sugar
1 cup brown sugar, packed
2 large eggs
$1^1/_2$ teaspoons vanilla
3 cups gluten-free almond blend flour
1 teaspoon baking soda
1 teaspoon sea salt
$^1/_4$ teaspoon xanthan gum
1 package semi-sweet chocolate chips

Directions:

Preheat oven to 375° F. Line cookie sheets with a baking mat or parchment paper.

Cream together the butter and sugars in a large mixing bowl. Mix in eggs (one at a time) and vanilla until blended.

Sift together flour, baking soda, sea salt and xanthan gum in a medium size bowl. Add flour mixture to wet mixture and mix about 2 minutes or until thoroughly combined. Stir in chocolate chips. Drop by rounded teaspoonful on baking sheets about 2-inches apart.

Bake for 10 to 12 minutes or until light brown. Let rest 5 minutes on baking sheets and then remove to cool completely on wire racks.

Coconut Macaroons

These cookies can be made ahead and stored in an airtight container for two weeks or in the freezer for one month.

Makes $3^1/_2$ to 4 dozen cookies

Ingredients:

3 egg whites
$^1/_4$ teaspoon cream of tartar
$^1/_8$ teaspoon sea salt
$^3/_4$ cup cane sugar
$^1/_4$ teaspoon almond extract
2 cups flaked coconut
3 drops red or green food coloring, optional

Directions:

Preheat oven to 350° F.

Beat egg whites, cream of tartar and salt in a large bowl until foamy. Beat in sugar, **1 tablespoon at a time**. Continue beating until stiff and glossy. Do not under beat. Fold in almond extract, coconut and food color.

Drop mixture by teaspoonful about 1-inch apart on a baking sheet lined with parchment paper. Bake until edges are light brown, 20 to 25 minutes. Cool 10 minutes and remove from baking sheet.

Bridget's Cookie Tip: *If cookie tops do not brown properly, move baking sheet to a higher rack for the last couple minutes of baking.*

Cran-Orange Cookies

These flavorful drop cookies are wonderful for holiday treats.

Makes about 3 to 4 dozen cookies

Ingredients:

$1^1/_3$ cups cranberries, fresh or frozen
$1^1/_4$ cups plus 3 tablespoons brown sugar, divided
$1^3/_4$ cups gluten-free almond blend flour
$1^1/_2$ teaspoons ground cinnamon
$^3/_4$ teaspoon ground coriander
$^3/_4$ teaspoon baking soda
Heaping $^1/_4$ teaspoon ground cloves
$^1/_4$ teaspoon sea salt
$^1/_8$ teaspoon xanthan gum
1 cup unsalted butter, softened
2 large eggs
$1^1/_2$ tablespoons light corn syrup
$1^1/_2$ teaspoons vanilla extract
$1^1/_2$ teaspoons grated orange zest
$1^2/_3$ cups old-fashioned oats, gluten-free

Directions:

Preheat oven to 350° F. Line baking sheets with a baking mat or parchment paper.

Using a food processor or blender, coarsely chop cranberries. Combine chopped cranberries and 3 tablespoons of brown sugar in a small bowl. Set aside.

Sift the flour, cinnamon, coriander, baking soda, cloves, salt and xanthan gum in a medium size bowl. Set aside.

Mix together butter and remaining brown sugar in a large bowl until well blended and creamy. Beat in eggs, one at a time. Beat in corn syrup, vanilla and orange zest until light and fluffy. Beat in the flour mixture. Fold in cranberry mixture and oats until combined. Drop by tablespoon onto baking sheets.

Bake cookies for 11 to 14 minutes, or until light brown on top. Let cookies rest for 3 minutes before removing cookies to wire rack to finish cooling.

"Life is short. Eat cookies for breakfast."

Dark Chocolate Chip Cookies

Moist and chewy, these cookies are perfect for the dark chocolate lover!

Makes 4 dozen cookies

Ingredients:

1 cup unsalted butter, softened
$^3/_4$ cup cane sugar
$^3/_4$ cup brown sugar, packed
2 large eggs
2 teaspoons vanilla extract
$2^1/_4$ cups gluten-free almond blend flour
1 teaspoon baking soda
$^1/_2$ teaspoon sea salt
$^1/_8$ teaspoon xanthan gum
2 cups Cacao (60%) chocolate chips, gluten-free

Directions:

Preheat oven to 375° F. Line baking sheets with a baking mat or parchment paper.

Cream the butter and sugars together in a large mixing bowl. Add in eggs, one at a time. Mix in vanilla extract.

Sift together flour, baking soda, sea salt and xanthan gum in a separate bowl. Gradually blend dry mixture into the creamed mixture. Stir in chocolate chips. Drop by tablespoon onto cookie sheets.

Bake 9 to 11 minutes or until golden brown. Let sit 5 minutes before removing to wire racks to cool completely.

Grandma's Oatmeal Cookies

I love filling the cookie jar with old-fashioned oatmeal cookies. They are delicious packed for lunches or a healthy afternoon snack.

Makes about 3 dozen cookies

Ingredients:

1 cup unsalted butter, softened
$^3/_4$ cups brown sugar, packed
$^1/_2$ cup cane sugar
1 egg
1 teaspoon vanilla extract
1 cup gluten-free almond blend flour
1 teaspoon baking soda
1 teaspoon ground cinnamon
$^1/_2$ teaspoon sea salt
$^1/_8$ teaspoon ground nutmeg
$^1/_8$ teaspoon xanthan gum
3 cups oats, gluten-free

Directions:

Preheat oven to 375° F. Line a baking sheet with a baking mat or parchment paper.

Mix together butter, sugar and egg in large size bowl until creamy. Add in vanilla extract.

Sift together flour, baking soda, cinnamon, sea salt, nutmeg and xanthan gum. Stir into wet mixture, blending well. Stir in oats. Drop dough by rounded teaspoons 2-inches apart on cookie sheet.

Bake 8 to 9 minutes. Remove from cookie sheet to cool on wire racks.

Iced Apple Cookies

Celebrate the arrival of fall by baking a huge batch of these delicious cookies. The tantalizing aroma of cinnamon, cloves and nutmeg will fill your home.

Makes about 3 dozen cookies

Ingredients:

2 cups gluten-free almond blend flour
1 teaspoon baking soda
1 teaspoon ground cinnamon
$1/2$ teaspoon Himalayan pink sea salt
$1/4$ teaspoon ground cloves
$1/4$ teaspoon ground nutmeg
$1/8$ teaspoon xanthan gum
$3/4$ cup unsalted butter, softened
$1^1/3$ cups light brown sugar
1 large egg
1 cup apple (Pink Lady or JonaGold,) peeled and chopped
$1/4$ cup apple cider

Directions:

Preheat oven to 350° F. Line baking sheets with a baking mat or parchment paper.

Sift together the flour, baking soda, cinnamon, salt, cloves, nutmeg and xanthan gum in a medium size bowl. Set aside.

Cream together the butter and sugar in a large bowl until light and fluffy. Add the egg and mix thoroughly. Gradually add the flour mixture and mix until combined. Stir in apples and apple cider. Drop by tablespoons on baking sheets.

Bake 18 to 22 minutes and remove from oven. Let cookies sit for 5 minutes before transferring to wire rack to finish cooling.

Apple Cider Icing

Ingredients:

3 cups confectioners' sugar
2 tablespoons unsalted butter, softened
2 to 3 tablespoons apple cider

Directions:

Combine the sugar, butter and apple cider in a small bowl. Stir until smooth. If frosting is too thick, add one teaspoon of apple cider until desired consistency is reached.

Frost cooled cookies. Let icing dry before stacking cookies.

Bridget's Cookie Tip: Bake cookies on center rack of oven.

Jo's No Bake Cookies

My mom used to make these cookies for my brothers. Now I enjoy making them for my family. They are one of my favorite cookies for summer.

Makes 3 dozen cookies

Ingredients:

$1^1/_2$ cups cane sugar
$^1/_2$ cup butter
$^1/_2$ cup whole milk or unsweetened nut milk
1 teaspoon vanilla extract
3 cups old-fashioned oats, gluten-free
1 cup shredded coconut
6 tablespoons cocoa (dark chocolate is my favorite)
$^1/_2$ cup cashew nuts

Directions:

Mix sugar, butter and milk into a 2-quart saucepan, stirring constantly. Bring to a boil for 1 minute. Remove from stove and add vanilla.

Combine the oats, coconut, cocoa and cashews in a large bowl. Pour hot mixture over dry ingredients and stir until thoroughly combined.

Drop by teaspoonful on parchment paper. Allow to dry.

"Cookies make hospitality easy."

Pumpkin Chocolate Chip Cookies

One of my favorite fall cookies! I love the taste of the pumpkin and dark chocolate together! They are chewy and delicious!

Makes about 5 dozen cookies

Ingredients:

1 cup unsalted butter, softened
1 cup light brown sugar, packed
1 cup cane sugar
2 large eggs
1 cup canned pumpkin
1 teaspoon vanilla extract
3 cups gluten-free flour blend
2 teaspoons baking soda
$1/2$ teaspoon salt
$1^1/2$ teaspoons ground cinnamon
$1/4$ teaspoon ground ginger
$1/4$ teaspoon ground nutmeg
$1/8$ teaspoon xanthan gum
2 cups Ghirardelli 60% cacao chips

Directions:

Preheat oven to 350° F. Line baking sheets with a baking mat or parchment paper.

Beat butter and sugars together in a large size bowl until creamy. Beat in eggs, one at a time. Mix in pumpkin and vanilla.

Sift together the dry ingredients in a separate bowl and mix into wet mixture. Stir in the chocolate chips. Drop by rounded teaspoons on baking sheets.

Bake 15 to 18 minutes or until edges are brown. Cool cookies for t minutes before moving them to finish cooling on wire racks.

Bridget's Baking Tip: *Always use quality ingredients in your cookie recipes to take them from ordinary to extraordinary!*

Sour Cream Drops

One of grandma's blue ribbon favorites!

Makes about 5 dozen cookies

Ingredients:

$1/2$ cup shortening, softened
$1^1/2$ cups cane sugar
2 large eggs
1 cup sour cream
1 teaspoon vanilla extract
$2^3/4$ cups gluten-free almond blend flour
$1/2$ teaspoon baking soda
$1/2$ teaspoon baking powder
$1/2$ teaspoon sea salt
$1/8$ teaspoon xanthan gum

Directions:

Mix together shortening, sugar and eggs together in a large bowl. Stir in sour cream and vanilla extract.

Sift together flour, baking soda, baking powder, sea salt and xanthan gum. Stir in to wet mixture. **Chill at least one hour before baking.**

Preheat oven to 400° F. Line baking sheets with a baking mat or parchment paper.

Drop rounded teaspoonful on baking sheets. Bake 8 to 10 minutes or until light brown. Remove and cool completely on wire racks.

Oatmeal Raisin Cookies

This gluten-free recipe would make grandma proud! Nutmeg adds just the right amount of warmth to these chewy cookies.

Makes about 4 dozen cookies

Ingredients:

1 cup unsalted butter, softened
1 cup light brown sugar, packed
$1/2$ cup cane sugar
2 large eggs
1 teaspoon vanilla extract
$1^1/2$ cups gluten-free almond blend flour
1 teaspoon baking soda
1 teaspoon ground cinnamon
$1/2$ teaspoon ground nutmeg
$1/2$ teaspoon sea salt
$1/8$ teaspoon xanthan gum
3 cups rolled oats, gluten-free
$1^1/2$ cups golden raisins

Directions:

Preheat oven to 350° F. Line cookie sheets with a baking mat or parchment paper.

Cream together the butter and sugars in a large bowl. Add in one egg a time until blended. Mix in vanilla until smooth.

Sift together the flour, baking soda, cinnamon, nutmeg, salt and xanthan gum. Stir into sugar mixture. Stir in oats and raisins. Drop by rounded teaspoonful onto cookie sheets.

Bake 10 to 12 minutes until light and golden. Let cool for 2 minutes before removing to wire racks to cool completely.

Cookie Packing
Tips For Mailing

~ Avoid fragile cookies. Choose hearty and bar cookies.

~ Wrap cookies separately or bottoms together. Keep crisp cookies separate from moist cookies.

~ Line a sturdy container, like a small cardboard box, add packing materials (bubble wrap, crumpled waxed or parchment paper). Carefully nestle the cookies inside the container, and seal with tape or tie tightly with ribbon.

~Place the container in a heavyweight cardboard shipping box. Add enough crumpled newspaper, bubble wrap, or foam peanuts to prevent the container from shifting. Write "fragile" and "perishable" on all sides of the box.

Sweet Sugar Cookies

Take a step back in time with these easy to make cookies. No frosting is needed on these easy to make delights.

Makes about 3 dozen cookies

Ingredients:

$1/2$ cup unsalted butter, softened
$1/2$ cup cane sugar
1 large egg
1 teaspoon vanilla extract
$1^{1}/_{8}$ cups gluten-free almond blend flour
$1/2$ teaspoon sea salt
$1/4$ teaspoon baking soda
$1/8$ teaspoon xanthan gum

Directions:

Preheat oven to 350° F. Line a baking sheet with a baking mat or parchment paper.

Cream butter, sugar, egg and vanilla extract together in a large bowl.

Sift together the flour, salt, baking soda and xanthan gum. Stir into wet mixture until blended. Drop by rounded teaspoonful on baking sheet.

Bake until delicately brown. Cookies will be soft. Cool slightly before removing from baking sheet.

"Some days you just need a cookie."

Summer's Pumpkin Cookies

Full of chewy, spicy goodness, these pumpkin cookies are wonderful for celebrating autumn.

Makes about 5 dozen cookies

Ingredients:

$^1/_2$ cup unsalted butter, softened
$1^1/_2$ cups cane sugar
1 large egg
1 cup pumpkin
1 teaspoon vanilla extract
$2^1/_2$ cups gluten-free almond blend flour
1 teaspoon baking powder
1 teaspoon baking soda
2 teaspoons ground cinnamon
$^1/_2$ teaspoon ground nutmeg
$^1/_2$ teaspoon ground cloves
$^1/_2$ teaspoon salt
$^1/_4$ teaspoon xanthan gum

Directions:

Preheat oven to 350° F. Line baking sheets with a baking mat or parchment paper.

Cream together butter and sugar in a large bowl. Beat in egg, pumpkin and vanilla until creamy.

Sift together dry ingredients in small bowl. Gradually mix in the wet ingredients, until thoroughly blended. Drop by rounded teaspoons on to parchment paper-lined baking sheets.

Bake for 15 to 18 minutes. Cool on baking sheets for 5 minutes and remove to wire racks to cool completely. Frost these cookies with cream cheese frosting on next page.

Cream Cheese Frosting II

Rich and creamy, this frosting is perfect for all of your cookies calling for icing!

Ingredients:

2 cups confectioners' sugar, sifted
2 tablespoons butter, softened
1 teaspoon vanilla extract
1-3 tablespoons milk
1 ounce cream cheese

Directions:

Combine sugar, butter, vanilla and 1 tablespoon of milk in a large bowl. Beat until smooth. Gradually add in more milk, 1 teaspoon at a time, until desired consistency is reached. This is a thick frosting not a glaze.

Frost each cookie and allow icing to harden before stacking on a plate or in cookie jar.

Bridget's Cookie Tip: *Frost cookies like a pro. Place 1 teaspoon of icing on the center of the cookie. With a spatula or knife, spread icing in a circular motion creating pretty swirls.*

Vanilla Wafers

Soft, chewy, and rich in vanilla flavor; they are wonderful in pudding desserts and cookie pie crusts.

Makes about 3 dozen

Ingredients:

$1^1/_3$ cups gluten-free almond blend flour
$^3/_4$ teaspoon baking powder
$^1/_4$ teaspoon sea salt
$^1/_8$ teaspoon xanthan gum
$^1/_2$ cup unsalted butter, softened
1 cup cane sugar
1 egg
1 tablespoon vanilla extract

Directions:

Preheat oven to 350° F. Line a baking sheet with a baking mat or parchment paper.

Sift together flour, baking powder, salt and xanthan gum in a medium bowl. Set aside.

Beat butter and sugar together in a large mixing bowl until creamy. Add in egg and vanilla, mix thoroughly. Beat in flour mixture, one cup at a time.

Drop by rounded teaspoons onto prepared baking sheets. Bake 12 minutes for a chewy cookie or 15 minutes for a crisp cookie. Remove from oven and let rest on cookie sheet about 5 minutes. Move cookies to wire rack and cool completely.

White Chocolate Cranberry Cookies

Easy to make, these festive cookies are crisp on the outside and chewy on the inside.

Makes 3 dozen cookies

Ingredients:

$2/3$ cup unsalted butter, softened
$2/3$ cup brown sugar, packed
2 large eggs
$1^1/2$ cups gluten-free almond flour blend
1 teaspoon baking soda
1 teaspoon sea salt
$1/8$ teaspoon xanthan gum
$1^1/2$ cups old-fashioned oats, gluten-free
$2/3$ cup dried cranberries, rinsed and drained
$2/3$ cup white chocolate chips

Directions:

Preheat oven to 375° F. Line two baking sheets with silicone mat or parchment paper.

Beat butter and sugar in a large size bowl until light and creamy. Add eggs, one at a time, mixing well.

Sift together flour, baking soda, salt and xanthan gum in a medium bowl. Add to butter and sugar mixture, mixing well. Mix in oats. Stir in cranberries and white chocolate. Drop by rounded teaspoon on prepared baking sheets.

Bake for 10 to 12 minutes or until golden brown. Remove from oven and let cookies rest for 5 minutes on cookie sheet before removing to wire rack.

White Chocolate Strawberry Shortcake Cookies

White chocolate and strawberries are amazing together in these soft and chewy cookies.

Makes about 3 dozen cookies

Ingredients:

$1/2$ cup unsalted butter, softened
1 cup sugar
1 egg, beaten
1 tablespoon heavy cream
$1 1/2$ teaspoons vanilla extract
2 cups gluten-free almond flour blend
1 teaspoon baking powder
$1/2$ teaspoon salt
$1/8$ teaspoon xanthan gum
1 cup white chocolate chips
$1/2$ cup fresh strawberries, washed, rinsed and chopped

Directions:

Preheat oven to 350° F. Line baking sheets with a baking mat or parchment paper.

Cream together the butter, sugar, egg, cream and vanilla in a large mixing bowl.

Sift together the flour, baking powder, salt and xanthan gum. Add to cream mixture and mix well. Stir in white chocolate chips and strawberries. Drop by rounded teaspoon.

Bake on parchment lined cookie sheets about 10-12 minutes, or until edges are lightly brown. Let cool for a few minutes before removing to a wire rack to cool completely.

Sugar Cookie Decorating Tips

~ Make dough & chill for at least 24 hours before cutting into shapes.

~ Refrigerate cut cookies for 30 minutes before baking to keep their shape.

~ Use royal icing to decorate cookies.

~ Add sprinkles within 2 minutes of frosting cookies.

~ Let frosting harden on cookies for 4 hours before storing.

ROLLED COOKIES

Snickerdoodles

Jam Thumbprints

Molasses Cutouts

Flourless Peanut Butter

"Nothing says home like the smell of baking."

Royal Icing Recipe

1 box (1 lb) Confectioners' sugar
5 Tablespoons meringue powder
Scant 1/2 cup warm water

Combine sugar and meringue powder in a large mixing bowl. (If using stand mixer, use the paddle attachment.) Add water. Beat on low speed until icing is smooth.

For a thinner consistency, used for flooding, add more water.

A thicker consistency is used for outlining and details.

Creamy Butter Cookies

Rich in flavor, these cookies are wonderful with a cup of hot tea or coffee.

Makes about 4 dozen cookies

Ingredients:

1 cup unsalted butter, softened
$1^1/_2$ cups confectioners' sugar
1 teaspoon vanilla extract
1 large egg
$2^1/_4$ cups gluten-free almond blend flour
1 teaspoon baking soda
1 teaspoon cream of tartar
$^1/_4$ teaspoon salt
$^1/_8$ teaspoon xanthan gum
Colored sanding sugar

Directions:

Preheat oven to 350° F. Line cookie sheets with a baking mat or parchment paper.

Mix butter, confectioners' sugar and vanilla in a large bowl until just blended. Add in egg and mix well.

Sift the flour, baking soda, cream of tartar, salt and xanthan gum in a medium size bowl. Add to the butter mixture and mix until well combined.

Shape dough into 1-inch balls and place 1-inch apart on baking sheets. Flatten each ball with a fork. Sprinkle with colored sanding sugar.

Bake until edges are light in color, about 8 to 10 minutes. Cool on baking pans for 5 minutes and then transfer to wire racks to finish cooling.

Jam Thumbprint Cookies

These easy drop cookies are my husband's favorite for Christmas. I fill them with raspberry or pomegranate jam.

Makes about 3 dozen cookies

Ingredients:

$1/2$ cup unsalted butter, softened
1 cup cane sugar
1 egg, slightly beaten
1 tablespoon heavy cream
1 teaspoon vanilla extract
2 cups gluten-free almond blend flour
1 teaspoon baking powder
$1/2$ teaspoon sea salt
$1/8$ teaspoon xanthan gum
$1/3$ cup favorite jam (raspberry, pomegranate, strawberry)
1 cup vanilla baking chips, if desired

Directions:

Preheat oven to 350° F. Line baking sheets with a baking mat or parchment paper.

Cream together the butter and sugar in a large bowl until light and fluffy. Add in egg, cream and vanilla; mixing well.

Sift together flour, baking powder, salt and xanthan gum in a medium size mixing bowl. Add to cream mixture and mix well.

Roll dough into $3/4$-inch balls and place 2-inches apart on baking sheet. Using your thumb or handle of a wooden spoon, gently create an indentation in the center of each cookie. Spoon or pipe about $1/4$ teaspoon of jam into each indentation.

Bake 8 to 10 minutes or until edges are golden brown. Cool 5 minutes; remove from cookie sheets to cooling rack.

Melt vanilla chips in a double boiler, stirring constantly until smooth. Spoon melted chips into a sealable food bag and cut a small hole in corner of bag. Gently squeeze bag to drizzle melted chips over cookies.

Bridget's Cookie Tip: *Chilling the dough makes it easier to handle.*

Flourless Almond Cookies

With only three ingredients, these cookies are a breeze to make.

Makes 2 dozen cookies

Ingredients:

1 cup cane sugar
1 cup almond butter
1 egg, slightly beaten

Directions:

Preheat oven to 350° F. Line baking sheets with a baking mat or parchment paper.

Beat sugar, almond butter and egg in a large bowl until smooth.

Shape dough into 24 balls, place 2-inches apart on cookie sheets. Flatten slightly with a fork.

Bake 10 minutes or until set. Transfer to wire rack and cool completely.

Bridget's Cookie Tip: *Make cookies special by dipping an end in melted chocolate.*

Flourless Peanut Butter Cookies

Imagine peanut butter cookies made without flour that taste especially good. I love how fast they are to make.

Makes 2 dozen cookies

Ingredients:

1 egg, slightly beaten
1 cup brown sugar, packed
1 cup organic peanut butter, smooth or chunky
1 cup chocolate chips, optional

Directions:

Preheat oven to 350° F. Line a baking sheet with a silicone mat or parchment paper.

Beat egg, brown sugar and peanut butter in a medium bowl with mixer until blended and smooth.

Shape dough into 24 balls; place 2-inches apart on cookie sheets. Flatten slightly with a fork.

Bake 10 to 12 minutes or until set. After removing from oven, let stand for 5 minutes and transfer to wire rack; cool completely.

Melt chocolate chips in a double boiler over low heat and drizzle over cookies. Spoon melted chips into a sealable food bag and cut a small hole in corner of bag. Gently squeeze bag to drizzle melted chips over cookies. Allow chocolate to cool completely before stacking.

Gingersnaps

Crisp on the outside and chewy on the inside, you will love these spicy cookies with a glass of cold milk.

Makes 2 dozen cookies

Ingredients:

1 cup brown sugar, packed
$3/4$ cup shortening
$1/4$ cup molasses
1 large egg
$2 1/4$ cups gluten-free almond blend flour
2 teaspoons baking soda
1 teaspoon ground cinnamon
1 teaspoon ground ginger
$1/2$ teaspoon ground cloves
$1/4$ teaspoon salt
$1/8$ teaspoon xanthan gum
1 cup cane sugar, add more if needed

Directions:

Mix brown sugar, shortening, molasses and egg in a large bowl. Sift together flour, baking soda, cinnamon, ginger, cloves, salt and xanthan gum. Stir into wet mixture. **Cover and refrigerate at least 1 hour.**

Preheat oven to 375° F. Line baking sheets with a baking mat or parchment paper.

Shape dough by rounded teaspoonful into balls. Dip tops in cane sugar. Place balls, sugar sides up on a baking sheet. Sprinkle a few drops of water on cookies before baking to give you an old-fashioned cracked top.

Bake cookies until set, about 10 to 12 minutes.

Molasses Cutouts

These spicy cutouts are super cute! They freeze well too!

Makes about 3 dozen cookies

Ingredients:

$^2/_3$ cup shortening
$1^1/_2$ cups cane sugar
2 large eggs
2 tablespoons buttermilk
2 tablespoons molasses
$3^1/_2$ cups gluten-free almond blend flour
1 teaspoon sea salt
1 teaspoon baking soda
1 teaspoon baking powder
1 teaspoon ground ginger
$^1/_2$ teaspoon ground cloves
$^1/_4$ teaspoon xanthan gum
Confectioners' sugar, sanding sugar, or sprinkles, if desired

Directions:

Cream together the shortening and sugar in a large bowl until light and fluffy. Beat in eggs, buttermilk, and molasses.

Sift together flour, salt, baking soda, baking powder, ginger, cloves and xanthan gum in a medium size bowl. Gradually beat into creamed mixture.

Divide dough in half and shape each into a round disk. Wrap in plastic wrap. **Refrigerate 4 hours or overnight.**

Preheat oven to 375° F. Line cookie sheets with a baking mat or parchment paper.

Roll dough to $^1/_8$-inch thickness on a lightly floured surface or on parchment paper. Cut with a floured 3-inch cookie cutter. Place 2-inches apart on baking sheets.

Bake 8 to 10 minutes or until edges are brown. Remove from baking sheets to wire racks to cool completely. Decorate as desired.

Bridget's Cookie Tip: If cutouts are soft after cutting out, refrigerate for about 10 minutes. Gently transfer to baking sheet.

Mom's Sugar Cookies

This old-fashioned recipe was originally called sugar thins and has been passed down through my husband's family. I was honored when my mother-in-law passed it on to me. I loved finding these gems in her cookie jar!

Makes 2-4 dozen cookies

Ingredients:

1 cup cane sugar
$1/2$ cup unsalted butter, softened
1 egg, beaten
1 tablespoon heavy whipping cream
1 teaspoon vanilla extract
2 cups gluten-free almond blend flour
1 teaspoon baking powder
$1/2$ teaspoon salt
$1/8$ teaspoon xanthan gum

Directions:

Cream together butter and sugar in a large mixing bowl until light and fluffy. Add in egg, cream and vanilla; mixing well.

Sift together flour, baking powder and sea salt in a medium size mixing bowl. Add to cream mixture and mix well. Wrap dough in plastic wrap and **refrigerate two hours or overnight.**

Preheat oven to 350° F. Line a baking sheet with a baking mat or parchment paper.

Roll out dough in a small quantity, on a slightly floured board, until very thin ($1/8$ -inch). Cut cookies out with small cookie cutters.

Bake for about 5 minutes. Cool cookies for 2 minutes before removing to cooling rack. Cool completely before icing with the sugar cookie glaze.

Sugar Cookie Glaze

This delicious glaze adds just the right amount of sweetness to cookies.

Ingredients:

1 cup confectioners' sugar, sifted
$1^1/_2$ tablespoons whole milk
1 teaspoon vanilla extract
Food coloring, optional

Directions:

Mix sugar, milk and vanilla in a medium size bowl until thoroughly blended. Add food coloring in one drop at a time, until desired color is achieved. For a thinner glaze, add $^1/_2$ teaspoon of milk at a time until desired consistency is reached. "Paint" glaze on with a pastry brush.

Bridget's Cookie Tip: *Sugar cookies are wonderful for all occasions. Use heart shaped cookie cutters for Valentine's Day, flower shaped cookie cutters for Mother's Day, and rabbit cookie cutters for Easter.*

Russian Teacakes

A favorite for the holidays, these gems are perfect for a cookie exchange.

Makes about 4 dozen cookies

Ingredients:

1 cup unsalted butter, softened
2 cup confectioners' sugar
1 teaspoon vanilla extract
$2^{1}/_{4}$ cups gluten-free almond blend flour
$^{3}/_{4}$ teaspoon salt
$^{1}/_{8}$ teaspoon xanthan gum
$^{3}/_{4}$ cup finely chopped nuts

Directions:

Preheat oven to 400° F. Line a baking sheet with a baking mat or parchment paper.

Mix butter, $^{1}/_{2}$ cup confectioners' sugar and vanilla extract in a large bowl until creamy.

Sift together flour, salt, xanthan gum and nuts in a medium size bowl. Stir into wet ingredients until dough holds together. Shape into 1-inch balls. Place about 1-inch apart on cookie sheet.

Bake about 10 to 12 minutes or until set. Roll in remainder of confectioners' sugar while warm; cool. Roll in confectioners' sugar again.

"Baking cookies is a great way to create long-lasting memories and family traditions."

Shortbread Cutouts

For a sparkling treat, sprinkle white sanding sugar on top of these cookies.

Makes 4 dozen cookies

Ingredients:

4 cups gluten-free almond blend flour
1 cup confectioners' sugar
$1/4$ teaspoon salt
$1/8$ teaspoon xanthan gum
4 sticks cold butter (cut into $1/2$-inch cubes)

Directions:

Preheat oven to 350° F. Line cookie sheets with a baking mat or parchment paper.

Sift together flour, sugar, salt and xanthan gum in a large bowl. Add butter and mix on low until dough sticks together.

Roll the dough on a lightly floured board or parchment paper, to $1/4$-inch thick. Cut out with your favorite cookie cutters. Arrange 1-inch apart on cookie sheets. **Prick each cookie with a fork.** Sprinkle lightly with sanding sugar.

Bake for 10 to 15 minutes or until light brown. Let cookies cool on cookie sheets for 5 minutes then transfer to wire rack to cool.

Bridget's Baking Tip: *To prevent fork from sticking to cookie dough, dip it in confectioners' sugar.*

Snickerdoodles

Create childhood memories with these fun cookies.

Makes about 3 dozen cookies

Ingredients:

1 cup unsalted butter, softened
1 1/2 cups cane sugar plus 2 tablespoons
2 large eggs
2 3/4 cups gluten-free almond blend flour
2 teaspoons cream of tartar
1 teaspoon baking soda
1/2 teaspoon salt
1/8 teaspoon xanthan gum
2 teaspoons ground cinnamon

Directions:

Mix together butter, 1 1/2 cups sugar, and eggs in a large bowl.

Sift together flour, cream of tartar, baking soda, salt and xanthan gum. Stir in to creamed mixture until blended. **Chill dough for at least 2 hours or overnight.**

Preheat oven to 350° F. Line baking sheets with a baking mat or parchment paper.

Mix remaining sugar and cinnamon together in a small bowl. Roll dough into balls. Roll balls into cinnamon sugar mixture. Place on baking sheets.

Bake 8 to 10 minutes or until lightly browned. Remove to wire racks to cool.

Christmas Cookie Exchange Tips

~ Send invites out 3-4 weeks in advance. Include a RSVP on invitation.

~ Ask each guest to bake a dozen of cookies per person attending, plus an extra dozen for sampling.

~ Coordinate what cookies everyone will bring so you do not have duplicates. Ask attendees to include the recipe.

~ Set up a display table with name cards of each cookie.

~ Provide non-sweet snacks (cheese and crackers, veggies and dip, etc.) for guests to snack on.

~ Create a packaging table with saran wrap, resealable plastic bags and aluminum foil for guests to take home their goodies.

Pressed Cookies

Sparkling Snowflakes

Anise Tea Cookies

It's so easy to create fancy cookie designs and shapes using a cookie press.

Hot Chocolate Viennese

1/3 cup unsweetened cocoa powder
1/3 cup cane sugar
2 ½ cups milk
1 ½ cups freshly brewed coffee or espresso

~ Combine the cocoa powder and sugar in a medium saucepan. Press out any lumps.

~ Stirring constantly, pour ½ cup of milk into mixture; whisk in the coffee and remaining 2 cups of milk.

~ Over moderately low heat, cook, stirring occasionally, until mixture steams but does not boil. About 8 to 10 minutes.

~ Pour the hot chocolate in mugs and serve.

Anise Tea Cookies

If you like licorice, you will love these dainty cookies.

Makes about 5 dozen cookies

Ingredients:

1 cup unsalted butter, softened
$^3/_4$ cup cane sugar
1 large egg
4 drops anise oil
1 tablespoon orange juice
$2^1/_2$ cups gluten-free almond blend flour
$^1/_2$ teaspoon sea salt
$^1/_4$ teaspoon baking powder
$^1/_8$ teaspoon xanthan gum

Directions:

Preheat oven at 375° F. Cream together the butter and sugar in a large bowl. Beat in egg, anise oil, and orange juice.

Sift together flour, sea salt, baking powder, and xanthan gum in a small bowl. Gradually blend into wet mixture. Fill cookie press.

Bake for 10 to 12 minutes. Remove immediately to wire racks to cool completely.

Bridget's Cookie Tip: *These cookies would be wonderful for a special friend's birthday or Mother's Day gift. Line a small basket with a decorative dish towel. Add a pretty mug or tea cup, tea bags, infused honey, and these sweet cookies.*

Cookie Gift Packaging Ideas

~ Stack cookies in vintage inspired tea tins. Add twine and a cute gift tag.

~ Line a basket with a pretty dish towel and fill with cookies. Wrap basket in cellophane wrapping paper. Tie with a pretty ribbon.

~ Stack cookies in glass mason jars. Write the recipe on a cute card, puncture a hole in card, insert ribbon and tie around lid.

~ Fill a decorative gift bag with tissue paper and cookies.

~ Line a decorative metal tin with parchment paper. Fill with cookies.

Snow Flakes

These sweet little cookies are delicious with a cup of hot chocolate.

Makes 5 to 6 dozen cookies

Ingredients:

1 cup unsalted butter, softened
3 ounces cream cheese, softened
1 cup cane sugar
1 large egg yolk
1 teaspoon vanilla
1 teaspoon grated orange peel
$2\frac{1}{2}$ cups gluten-free almond blend flour
$\frac{1}{2}$ teaspoon sea salt
$\frac{1}{4}$ teaspoon ground cinnamon
$\frac{1}{8}$ teaspoon xanthan gum

Directions:

Preheat oven to 350° F. Line baking sheets with a baking mat or parchment paper.

Cream butter, cream cheese and sugar in a large mixing bowl. Beat in egg yolk, vanilla and orange peel.

Sift together the flour, salt, cinnamon and xanthan gum. Stir into wet mixture.

Bake 12 to 15 minutes or until lightly browned. Remove at once to wire racks and cool completely.

Bridget's Baking Tip: *Homemade cookies make lovely Christmas gifts for friends and neighbors.*

Spritz Cookies

These holiday cookies are so pretty decorated with colored sanding sugar.

Makes about 5 dozen cookies

Ingredients:

1 cup unsalted butter, softened
$^1/_2$ cup cane sugar
2 large eggs
1 teaspoon vanilla extract
$2^1/_4$ cups gluten-free almond blend flour
$^1/_2$ teaspoon salt
$^1/_8$ teaspoon xanthan gum
Colored sanding sugar or nonpareils, if desired

Directions:

Preheat oven to 400° F. Line cookie sheets with a baking mat or parchment paper.

Mix together butter and sugar in a large bowl until creamy. Add in eggs and vanilla mixing until blended.

Sift together flour, salt and xanthan gum in a medium size bowl. Stir into wet mixture until blended. Place dough in cookie press. Press desired shapes on cookie sheets.

Bake until set about 7 to 10 minutes. Do not brown. Immediately remove from cookie sheet to cool on wire racks. Sprinkle with colored sugar or nonpareils, if desired.

Written by Bridget Towery

Your Gluten-Free Holiday Dessert Tray

Your Gluten-Free Pie Tin - Coming 2018

www.bakingwithbridget.com

Made in the USA
San Bernardino, CA
18 April 2019